Bringing Flames to your Fingertips

Doug Stults
Simi Valley, California, USA

WARNING!

Fire is useful, beautiful and dangerous.

If you abuse the information in this guide by firemaking in foolish places at foolish times with few precautions....

Don't even think about trying to hold us liable.

Printed in the United States of America.

First edition

Cover design by Doug Stults

Photographs by Lori Menke, Carrie Harlan and Doug Stults

ISBN 978-1-4303-2952-7

1. Survival Skills-Primitive-Friction Fire Making 2. Fire Making-Primitive-Techniques 3. Native Plants-Historical Use 4. Native American-Living Skills-United States-Southwest

This little guide is dedicated to my Mom and Dad...
for encouraging me to seek out my own answers and
inspiring me with the beauty of wilderness.

Photos by Doug Stults, Lori Menke and Carrie Harlan

TABLE OF CONTENTS

INTRODUCTION

First, this guide is not something you should read while lazily sipping a latte in some comfortable, air-conditioned coffee house so you can feel the vicarious thrill of making fire only in your imagination. Instead, it is a small guide designed to be taken in the field, crushed, spilled upon, drooled over, accidentally charred in your campfire and inadvertently dropped from your backpack as you hang off a huge fingernail biting cliff and washed downstream through the terror of class V rapids. Go ahead.... eat a fish off its cover or rip a few back pages out for TP. In other words, DO IT! Destroy these pages if done in the pure pursuit of experiencing the magic of creating fire!

So let's just jump right in.... When making fire you will need to have three things: the correct mind set - for example, a feeling of openness to the mysterious thing that is about to happen.... you need the correct materials.... oh, never mind this one - if you have the correct mind set, you will find something that will work! And lastly, you will need patience combined with practice... but trust me - once you create fire, and I mean you actually nurture it to life yourself... Gently holding the tinder in your sweaty palm, watching the smoke grow heavier and heavier and then.... flames suddenly leap from your fingertips.... well, your life will change! I know, I know - it sounds like I'm being melodramatic. But ask anyone who has ever accomplished this and I think you will find that they agree. Suddenly, this mysterious, sacred gift has now been earned by you. You will soar with confidence, like you just climbed the little known untouched peak next to Everest, as if you just crawled from the broiling desert into a shaded oasis, or, desperately clinging to a slippery, moss covered slab of crumbling shale and your foot just found a small crack to wedge into, or like paddling your leaking.... you see what I mean?

Anyway, on to the instruction.

I wish we could be together under an old cottonwood somewhere. That way I could do my best to see that you would have the most awesome experience. We might have hiked down a small creek, examining the holly leaf cherries (Are they ripe yet? Nope!), pausing momentarily to examine the scratches in the trail from coyotes, foxes, scrub jays, kangaroo rats, scorpions and blowing leaves.... By the time we arrived at our destination, our minds would be at ease, concerns and worries left behind. We would be fully immersed in the wild, being a part of, not apart from, the creatures and flora around us. We would be hot and tired and hungry.... exactly the sort of state you are likely to be in if you ever really needed to make your own fire. OK, enough of what I wish could be... Let's do fire.

Making fire..... somehow this rarest of skills is something that once mastered,...... scratch that...... one never masters firemaking. Each time it is tried, the outcome is unknown, a mysterious dance of knowledge, skill, respect and of course, Luck! For an activity with so many factors affecting the outcome, each success is a time for gratefully looking to the sky and offering a moment of thanks.

For those of us that just love exactness even when attempting a skill that doesn't require it, (Firemaking actually thrives of experimentation!) I will try to narrow the variables as much as possible and offer you a shopping list of tangible stuff to help in your fire making pursuit!

The Idea

The idea, of course, is to create friction - lots in some places and just a little in others. I know that sounds pretty easy.... who hasn't rubbed their hands together and been surprised at how much warmth they were able to generate from just that simple motion? (Or worse, had an older brother who enjoyed giving them "rug burns"!) But using a bunch of sticks, strings and grease to make fire turns this easy activity into a moderately difficult skill. You need to select the right kind of wood with the right moisture in them (or lack of moisture). The string must be strong but not tied on too tight. The back and forth motion that you use with the firebow is tough to consistently get right (When do I go faster? Harder? Am I sawing far enough? Too far?) and then you have to push down on the hand cup just.... the perfect...... amount... not too hard and not too light! And to make it even more difficult, this pressure has to change at different stages in the fire making process. Oh yeah, the tinder must be from the correct plant and roughed up enough to hold a spark but still let air in. And then there are similar considerations for the drill, the firebow, the kindling you will use and your early sticks for firewood to build the foundation of your fire..... are you getting discouraged? If so, that is normal. To write all the considerations down sounds like an impossible task but if you were to watch a firemaker create fire a couple of times and then try it yourself, you would see that so much of this is already inside your body and mind. You know this stuff; you just don't know that you know it!

First it sounded easy and now is sounds hard....
Don't worry - there really are many different materials that will work.... and
actually, it is this very abundance of possible firemaking supplies that
makes it a little bit harder. The trick is in finding out what works best with
the other materials that you are using.

The Complete Firemaking Kit

The Materials

From top to bottom in the photo above you see:

A **fireboard** - On the short side a fireboard is at least 4 inches long and 3/4 inches wide and 3/8 inches thick (hopefully you will be lucky enough to find one much longer... something like 9 inches long, 1 1/2 inches wide and 3/4 inches thick).

Fire drills in an assortment of lengths (from 4 1/2 to 9 1/2 inches) and thicknesses (3/8 to 1/2 inches).

A **firebow string** - about 4 1/2 feet long. Feel free to try any type of string (natural or otherwise). Although I like rawhide shoelaces, sinew, yucca, nettle and dogbane string will all work. Discover your own favorite one.... and learn to make it as well!

A **firebow** of around 30 inches long and 1/2 inch thick.

The **tinder bundle** is found to the left of center. It could be yucca, cottonwood or lots of other choices.... but my pick is the inner bark of a cottonwood tree.

And lastly, the three to the right of center are **hand cups**.... well greased! These should range from 5 inches long, 1 inch wide and 1/2 inch thick up to 9 inches long, 2 inches wide and 1 inch thick.

I have found a gazillion concrete suggestions while researching what type of wood you should use for the bow, drill and fireboard. In reality, try anything and everything that you want. Often, certain parts of a limb will work better than others or the piece of wood never mentioned in any book just feels like it might work. Go ahead - Try it! My favorite fireboard is one of oak, a wood that most firemakers and literature say is usually too hard to be a suitable fireboard.

Picture yourself on an unplanned overnight stay 400 years ago. If you couldn't find the plants that you were familiar with wouldn't you try just about any other plant that looked like it had similar characteristics as the wood you preferred? Yep, that's what I think too... so give it a go and learn from the experience! Look toward the end of this little guide for a couple of recommended types to try.

The Firebow

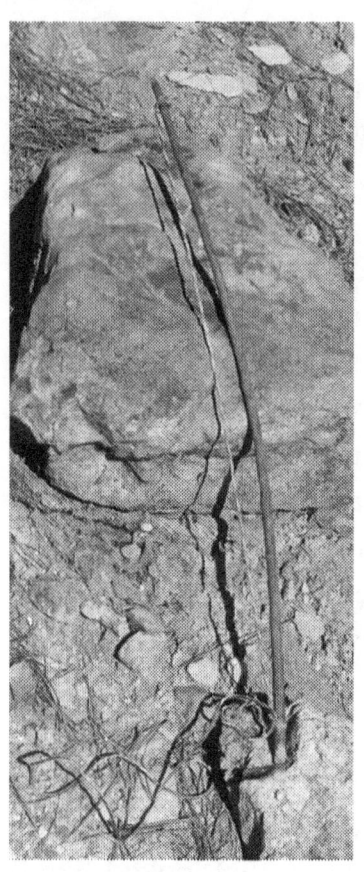

The Firebow

This piece of wood is about 30 inches long although you could use a shorter one.... or a longer one too. If you have a choice, go with the longer one as you can always trim it later. But the most important consideration is that it's long enough for you to get a full and controlled sweeping stroke (we will refer to this as "sawing" from here on out) when you are using it. Unfortunately, this is something that you will just have to try yourself to find out but I will describe the motion in fuller detail in a moment.

I prefer mulefat for my firebows. Mulefat grows in arroyos, gullies and streams around where I live in Southern California but it has a range from the eastern Sierras to San Diego.

Take a branch in both hands that is still growing on the bush. Can you bend it a just a little? It doesn't have to be super flexible, but enough to spring back to its original shape. If it does, then this looks like a great candidate for a firebow. Both ends of the bow will need to be prepared for the string. Each end will have a small shallow groove carved completely around the bow. To do this, I usually start by cutting a shallow ring all the way around the stick. *(photo 1)* Continue doing this all the way around the bow until you return to the spot you started at. Careful here! It's a lot harder than you think! You almost always tend to wrap around the stick and then end up WAY off from the beginning of your slice! I frequently stop and check that I am still circling the stick and not spiraling it!

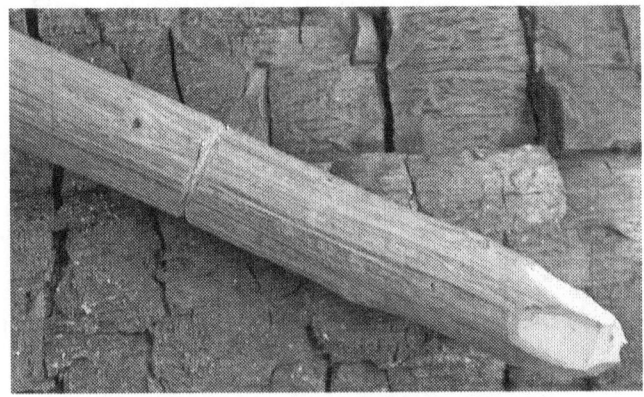

Photo 1 – Ringed Bow Tip

Photo 2 – Cutting the Bow Tip

This cut is so that later, in a few steps, I will be able to make a couple of additional passes and gradually cut deeper into the bow. I am then left with a clean edge that will hold the string securely. Next I start cutting off small chips of wood by working in from the end of the stick toward the middle very slowly and carefully so that I am able to stop at the ring when I get there.

Think whittling. *(photo 2)* I would also say that the total width of your groove should be about 3 to 4 times the width of the string you are going to be using. Repeat the steps above, again cutting a ring around the bow in the same spot as before but this time deeper. Again, slowly cut a small shaving of wood off using a very shallow angle of your knife. Start with the knife blade resting near one of the shallow ring cuts that you have made and then cut toward the ring, creating a narrowing groove encircling the bow. Don't go too deep! Again, you can always go too shallow, have the string slip off the first time you try to create fire, pause and cut the notch a little deeper. Once you've cut it off, you can't put it back on! Both of your finished bow ends should look like *photo 3*. A good bow like this can last for years even though it has dried out a bit and lost some of its spring. I have one I still use that has been around since 1989!

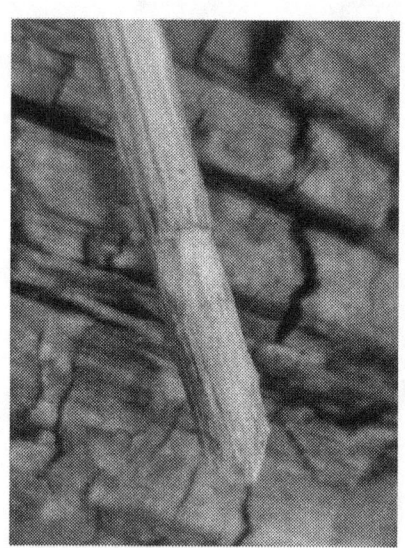

Choice Firebow Materials: Mulefat or Willow

SAWING is the full and controlled sweeping stroke of your arm just like sawing wood with an old fashioned bow saw.

Photo 3 - Finished Bow tip

The Drill

This piece of wood is probably going to be anywhere from 4 1/2 to 9 1/2 inches long. I find that using one shorter than this doesn't tend to work real well.... your hands don't have enough room for full controlled strokes and you seem to always end up hitting your carefully prepared tinder nest or bumping the fireboard or something else that you don't want to do. The drills I use are generally about 5 to 7 inches long and about 1/2 inch thick. They say that wider ones work a bit better as the outside perimeter of the drill is moving at a faster speed than a thin drill but I like to stick with thin drills.

Drills or Spindles

These are the tricky ones to find! You will invariably find a perfect deadfall branch, suitably dry and seemingly straight... and then when you get home, you see that it has an unpleasant bend, curve, knot, warp or twist to it that will make it totally useless for a drill. I would say.... DON'T WORRY ABOUT IT! It happens and you should get used to it.... don't ask me why, but I choose to view it as paying my dues. I figure that if I expend a bit of effort on drill selection and then realize upon closer inspection that I've just spent an afternoon collecting mostly firewood for a future Baja trip, so be it..... you should always be ready to pay a little to gain a lot!

So what you ought to look for is (Yep! You guessed it!) a straight branch! Look for one that is fairly close to the thickness you want (about 1/2 inch, remember?) but you may want to err on the side of picking one up that's a bit thicker than the final drill you envision. You should also start with deadfalls that lie in an open area. This way you will hopefully be looking at wood that has dried naturally and hasn't been lying in a shady spot just sucking up moisture. I don't believe that I have ever used a green branch to make a drill although I would not be extremely surprised if someone told me that they were actually successful in using one to make a fire. I just figure that I want as many odds in my favor that I can get so I always start with dry wood. I usually spend a great amount of time picking up huge branches (UGH!) and trying to look along the wood with my face near one end of the branch. I am trying to see any straight spots (Hmmmmm....) that seem to go on for a while. If I find a likely spot, I grab it with my hand and then bring it a lot closer to my eye. If it still looks straight, I will take it home. After you do this 10 or 15 times you will most likely have a pretty good selection so that even if 5 or 6 of them don't work, you still have enough variety to create a few good drills.

Now you are ready to turn this branch into a drill! Take your knife and cut as deep as you can around the wood in a circle. You may want to repeat this one more time and then just break it with your hands. If this is done correctly, it will break exactly where you have cut and the branch tip will be fairly close to the shape that you need also! Do this on both ends and now you are ready to fine-tune the drill. It is often at this stage that I see my drill is way out of whack. If it is just a bit off, I may try shaving off the uneven spot - sometimes you can get a drill to work even if it is not perfectly straight..... but it will probably be harder. If it looks straight you should proceed by roughly shaping the ends into cones by cutting with a knife or just rubbing it on a rock. Don't worry too much about making these perfect cones.... As you are using the drill it will reshape itself once it starts to bite and all the roughness will be gone - your drill will be sooooo smooth! The only thing I would concern myself with is the thickness of your drill compared to the thickness of your fireboard. If the hole you made (or will make) in the fireboard is too small for the drill, you will quickly come to a point where the drill is acting up unnecessarily as it starts to actually drill into the wood and begins cutting too far beyond the fireboard edge! We'll get into more of that in just a moment when we are choosing our fireboard.

Choice Drill Materials: Mulefat or Cottonwood

Keep a close eye on the drill.... if after using it a few times you see indentations or grooves around it, use a knife and carefully shave it back to round. You may also want to loosen how tight you tied your firebow string.

The String

The String

No real secret about the string.... you don't have too many choices here..... if you can't make your own string! If you can make your own string (And it really is a great skill to learn!), there are many suitable plants and materials out there - yucca, milkweed, stinging nettle, dogbane, sinew, hair or the skin of some deer. All of these will work but to create a strong durable string from them is way beyond the scope of this small guide. Someday.... yep.... someday, I will have another small book out here guiding you on the process of string making. In the meantime either go out and learn to make string from a friend or another book (Gotta love all this experimenting!) or try rawhide shoelaces. I know, I know.... it's cheating and all that and the purists out there have just ripped this guide in two. I happen to be of the opinion that when starting out with firemaking you shouldn't make things harder on yourself. It's difficult enough without trying to make your own string, and having to deal with making it really, really strong, even and flexible. Go ahead and give the shoestring a try.

Take a look at *photos 4, 5 and 6* on the next page. This is just a simple knot that I tied (basically a loop on the end of the string and then I fed the string through) to be placed in the notch you made earlier at the end of the bow furthest from your hand.

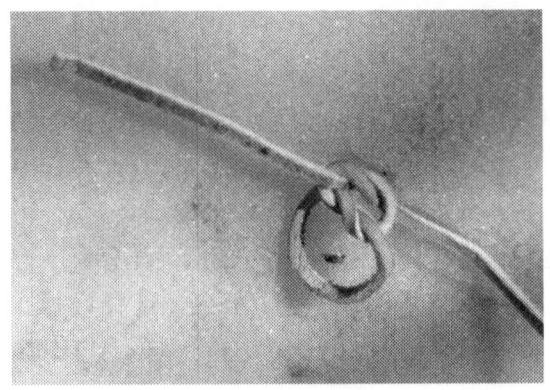

Photo 4
Just the Knot

Here you can see the circle in the string that you will feed the free end through.

Photo 5
Knot & loop

By feeding the free end through the small circle you have formed a slip knot.

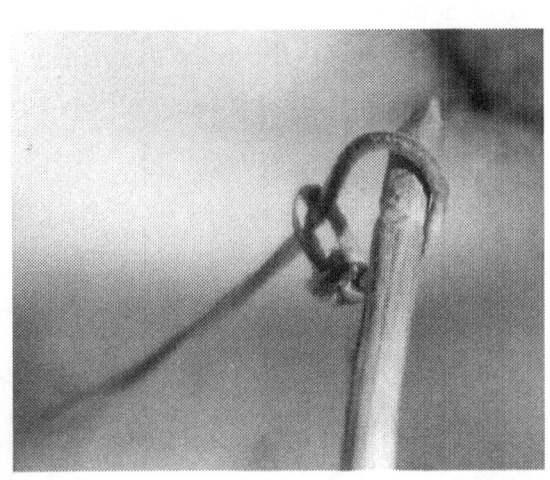

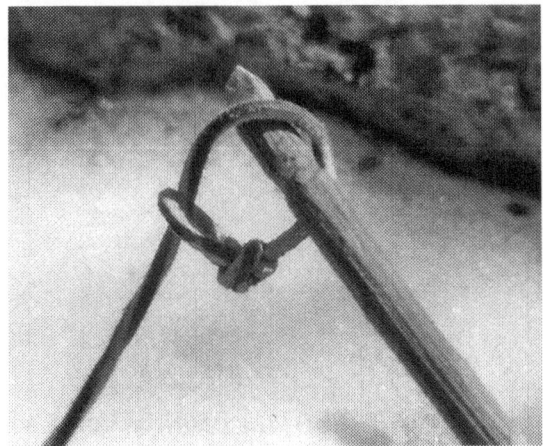

Photo 6
Another view

The slip knot is in the notch you made earlier and ready to be tightened!

I suppose that you could really put it on either end, but I like to hold the other knot with all its extra string in my hand. In *photo 7* you can see the knot that I have tied on the end (again in the notch), which will be in my hand. This is also a slip knot but of a different type than the first one. This one is simply a single square knot tied with the loose end stuck back under the knot. Then it is pulled tight as in *photo 8*. Now before you tie this last knot, put a little twist in the string - not so much twist that when you bring the ends of the string together that the whole thing starts to twist together.... just enough that there is a constant twist all the way down the string. Take a look at some of the photos showing the firebow for examples.

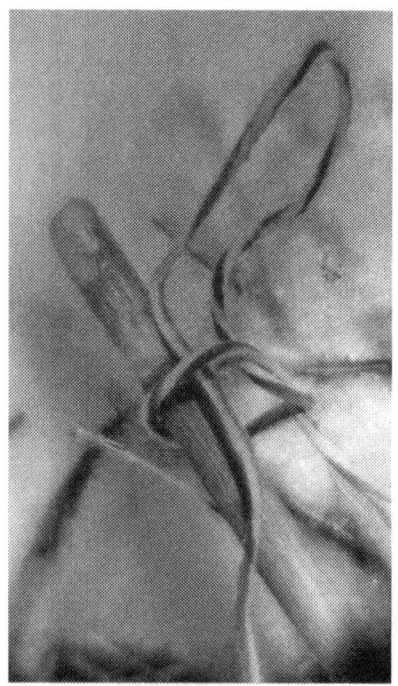

Photo 7
Slip knot near hand
(untightened)

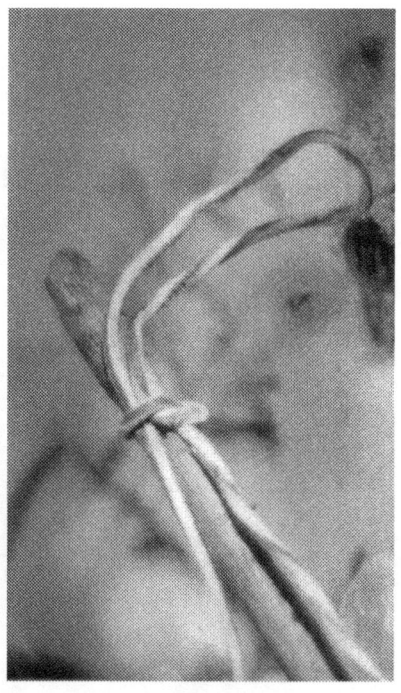

Photo 8
Slip knot near hand
(tightened)

When you think you are done with this stage, test your string. Your string should not be extremely taunt on the bow and the bow should not be bending much at all because of your string. Keep it barely tight and bending the bow just a bit. The way to test if you have enough tension is to properly place your drill in the string.... at this point you may want to skip forward to *photo 14* to see how to do this. If the string is so tight that when wrapping it around the drill you feel the bow REALLY bend and you almost can't do it.... it is WAY too tight. If you can hold the bow in one hand and with your other grab the drill and run it back and forth thru the string..... and I'm saying that the string is actually moving across the drill without moving the bow.... it is WAY too loose. What you want is a happy medium.... not too tight and not too loose..... and now you want to know when you have it just right, don't you? Well, guess what? You are now at another of those it's-just-a-feel-thing you have to experiment with. Some tips that I can give you are this: if the string starts to slip across the drill in the early stages of making fire.... by this I mean <u>before</u> you are getting powder in the hole...... your string is definitely too loose. Also in this early stage if you see very light grooves (see photos showing the drills) or indentations being pressed into your drill from the string, it is too tight and you will have to take the grooves out of the drill.

And lastly, don't get discouraged when, after just two or three passes of the bow, your string seems to have suddenly loosened up.... and I mean loosened up a bunch! Don't sweat it.... a new string ALWAYS stretches quite a bit and then you need to twist and tie it again to take up the slack.... and then you do two or three more passes and..... uh huh.... it has loosened up again! This may happen three or four times with a new string.... or maybe more. Very irritating but it will eventually tighten up and not change too much.

Choice String Materials: leather boot lace, Yucca, Dogbane

Lotsa string is good! You tend to break them often so a good backup supply is always necessary!

The Fireboard

The Fireboard

This piece of wood ought to be around 7 or 8 inches long and, of course, you could use a slightly longer or shorter one or even a really long one. But, having said this, the most important thing to look for when selecting your fireboard is that it is long enough for your foot (or your knee if you're one of those strange types) to hold it down securely. One thing above all others I think, that will really cause trouble when you try to make a fire is a wobbly fireboard! And, of course, you also need to have enough room for your hand to be sweeping back and forth and not so cramped when you're holding the drill against your shin. Oh yeah, and it should be dry. And I should also add that a gummy, sappy, green resinous branch fresh from the tree is probably not a good idea.... mmmm, no.... really, really not a good idea!

Now it's time to turn this branch into a good functional fireboard. First you have to shave a bit off the top so you have a flat surface and a little bit off the bottom for a flat surface. You'll also be shaving both edges more or less flat, turning your entire fireboard into a roughly rectangular shape. Of course you don't have to cut the ends... it's perfectly fine to leave them the way they are. Once you have a likely fireboard chosen and roughly shaped to the size you need, create a small dent or depression where you think your fire drill should have its hole. This is the tricky part! See *photo 9*. If you're too close to the edge, before you make very many fires or maybe even just one fire, your drill

Photo 9
Fireboard socket

will start to grind through to the outer edge of the fireboard and will continually pop out of the hole. If you go too far in, you will have to cut a huge notch to be able to reach the hole your fire drill is making and this will make it more likely for your coal to get jammed up and stuck inside the notch... Why is this bad you may ask? Because then you have to fiddle around trying to gently flick the coal out of the notch without destroying it.... very tricky indeed!

I know..... you're saying how am I supposed to know if the fireboard is too wide or too narrow? Too thin or too thick? The hole is too close to the edge or not? Well, all I can tell you is it's again one of those things you must practice and practice. After you do this a few times, you get the idea and learn what feels about right for this piece of wood today.

Choice Fireboard Materials: Cottonwood, Oak and Cedar.

Yucca, Juniper and Cottonwood Tinder

The Tinder Bundle

Can't forget this one! Now, lotsa stuff will work and lotsa stuff won't. I think the best way to find out is to experiment. By playing with it, I have come up with my own favorite recipe. I like a blend of the inner bark of the cottonwood tree (about 70% of the mix), juniper bark (around 10%), and a bit of old yucca fibers (the remaining 20%). And here is why - The cottonwood bark seems to be perfect and you could definitely stick with a tinder bundle of just this..... but the juniper bark seems a little harder to ignite and once the cottonwood starts to go, the juniper is next in line. Think of it as slowly adding thicker and thicker twigs to your fire so it burns a little slower giving time to build a bigger fire. The yucca seems to go up quick but won't last. I use this in there to help build up the heat and catch the flame a bit.

Start by folding a bunch of your preferred material into a little ball around 1/2 the size of your closed fist. I then hollow out a little pit in the middle of the tinder bundle and set it on the ground. Sift some of the smallest pieces of your material into the pit, creating a soft bed to receive the dust and ultimately, the coal.

Having said all this, I must restate: try anything out! I can't even begin to list all the different materials that I have tried.... but if it will burn..... mix it in there and see what happens!

Choice Tinder Bundle Materials: inner bark of **Cottonwood**

The Hand Cup

Wood & Stone Hand Cups

This is a pretty easy item to come up with... finally! Now some folks really like to go the easy route and use a shot glass.... It's true... It fits pretty good in the hand, it's sturdy and you don't have to worry about keeping the upper end of the drill well lubricated. BUT.... I'm fairly against using something so unnatural as a shot glass when natural materials are so easy found. Besides.... it just doesn't feel right! And don't forget that the fun factor is real high on this one because many people find it disgusting! Oh yeah!

First, all you really need is a small palm sized piece of wood with a small impression in it. Now it is true that you don't HAVE to have an impression or dent in it.... but then you will just have to make one. My theory is that if you can find it already done for you, why do it yourself? (This goes along with my firm belief that cutting firewood is just a waste of time if you can BURN it in half instead!) I like to make the impression fairly deep so the drill won't slip out.

Now... On to the gross part! The only thing you need now to turn your little old chunk of dented wood into a beautiful, functional speed demon of a hand cup is ...... grease! But where you get this grease is what makes the whole thing interesting! I like to take the end of the drill that will ALWAYS be in the hand cup and rub it along the side of my nose. That's right.... the side of my nose. No, I didn't say the inside of my nose...... it's the

SIDE of my nose! Believe it or not, you've got tons of high grade grease that is suitable right there.... just rub away making sure to get only the end of the drill and if you need more you always have the other side of your nose! Another trick is to rub it through your hair and even if you just washed your hair, you will still have enough grease in there to lube up the drill. The only thing to remember when doing this is that you should notice (or make a mark if you think you will forget) any identifying marks on the lubed up side of your drill. This way you will never.... and I mean NEVER put the wrong end into the fireboard.... doing this cardinal sin even once will mean a very, very long time before you will be getting fire from that hole! Worst case when you do this (And you will!) is that you get out your knife and scrape out the inside of the hole as best you can.... this way you remove some of the grease and hopefully enough clean wood is exposed to make the hole work again.

Nose grease supplier

Choice Hand Cup
Materials: Oak

Don't forget to make a very, very large clearing around your fire making location - Wind can always blow embers away extremely quickly so be ready! I like to keep lots of water nearby and have about 20 feet cleared on all sides!

The Technique

OK... now you have all your materials laid out and ready to go! You take a look around you and say "Hmmmm.... now what?".

Well, here is where we get into the "Now what?". Ready? Cool!

Photo 10 - Fireboard with tinder in position

After clearing a wide open area around the firemaking spot of other flammables, prepare the spot for the fireboard by digging a small hole and placing your tinder bundle into it.... try to place it so that when the powder is coming from the notch, it is fed right into the best spot in your tinder bundle. I often like to place a large leaf (Sycamore or maple are great!) or two in the hole first and then the tinder. See *photo 10*. Sometimes it helps when it comes time to remove the tinder from under the fireboard and you don't want to disturb the coal much.

Next, crouch down over the fireboard as seen in *photo 11* and on the cover. This position is the best because your leg can support the hand gripping the hand cup (Lock that hand to that shin! Think of your body melting together at that point and don't let it shift. Movement here can cause you lots and lots of trouble!). You are also able to press down with your entire body to

Photo 11 - Primo Crouching Position

increase friction at the contact point between the drill and fireboard. Your ability to regulate how much pressure you are applying is much better in this position than just using your arms to push down. Try it, you'll see! This is an important skill to get down... it just seems natural to want to push down harder with your arms and go quicker.... but resist this temptation and instead just shift your body weight .... lean in a bit more on the hand holding the cup on top of the drill. Now lean back to ease up on the pressure. Just a little pressure goes a long way! Practice this often and it will be easier for your body to remember. Also be sure you are not wearing clothing that tends to bind up your arms - you will need a full range of motion from your shoulders and arms for sawing on the fireboard.

Now, pick up the bow and get ready for the difficult trick of firebow handling! Of all the tricks to making fire, this has to be the one that will make or break it! Or at least it is one of two huge ones..... uh, I mean.... there are quite a few great tricks and this is just one of them..... But it's still important!

Photo 12
Little tension

Photo 13
Maximum tension

Look at the photos above and you can see my hand position on the bow.... (be prepared to study these photos for a while and try the positions out yourself because this is a bit tricky....) Notice how all the extra string is held inside my grip? That's a good thing! See how my fingers and thumb can create more tension *(photo 13)* on the string by gripping tighter and that by relaxing my fingers *(photo 12)* I can reduce the tension? I can't imagine NOT holding the firebow this way! Why, you may ask? Because as you are making fire you will find out that many things change... the string gets looser (Hey! Take up that slack!) and as you continue sawing, the drill meshing with the fireboard will cause a change in the ease of the sawing motion.

Suddenly you'll notice that it is getting harder to go back and forth and before you know it, your string is revolving around the drill but the drill isn't moving! Aarrgghh! Not only will you be losing heat but you will be indenting grooves around your drill that must be cut off (More heat loss!) before that drill will work again. Plus, all this is happening right when you are on the brink of making fire! (Why cut out the grooves? Cause now you have a bunch of high and low spots on your drill... you will never be able to control it with the constant slips and catches while you work!) By holding the bow the way I have shown, you will feel these things and be able to make immediate adjustments to the tension to compensate and keep things moving smoothly. Besides, at the very end you might like to finish it off with a grand display of energy (Any display of energy will be grand at that stage!) and saw back and forth furiously to spit the smoking coal out! You can't do that unless you have continual control of the string tension.

Now we'll focus on how to get that string wrapped around that drill. Fortunately, this is really not too hard. Take the drill and start on oh... let's say the right side of the string. With the greasy end pointing down, rotate the drill beneath the string to the left side and lift it up into an upright position without letting the string slip from the initial side of the drill. Now the greasy end is pointing up! Very important! See *photo 14* for the beginning position and *photo 15* for the final position ready to start firemaking! Another thing to keep in mind is if you want the drill wrapped on the inside of the firebow or the outside. I know, I know.... what is he talking about? Check out *photo 15* and you can see that the drill is wrapped to the outside of the firebow and string. If you want it on the inside (as I prefer), then just flip the drill over while still in the string. The greasy end is now on the top, right???? Make sure you check this!

Photo 14 - Loading the Drill

Photo 15 - Drill is ready

So, let's see.... fireboard is over the tinder and properly placed, we know the hand holding the hand cup needs to be locked against the shin (tight!) and the other will hold the bow with the extra string bundled up in the palm. OK, let's get those feet in order!

Check out *photo 11* again and notice how both your feet ought to be positioned. At this point I will guess that some of you will be using the bow in your right hand, just like me. For those lefties out there, just switch my "left foot" and "right foot" directions around and it will all work out!

Try out the body position with all the firemaking paraphernalia nearby and get ready to start. I like to kneel down for practice into a spot where I feel comfortable, look at where my knee is in the dirt and then get up and clean all the rocks, twigs, nails, broken glass and jagged hunks of metal out of the hollow my knee will be in. Somehow it just seems to make fire creation easier to have a clean spot for my knee and all that weight there! Next, the foot that is connected to the leg that will have your hand with the hand cup pressing against it (Whew! Should have just said "left foot"!) should go very close to the fireboard hole that you will be using... I would say about 1/2 inch from the side of the hole. And lastly, your knee and leg should NOT be encircled by your left arm when you press against your shin..... I've seen people do it this way but it just doesn't seem possible to be comfortable in that position or to bring enough pressure to bear on the fireboard! Try it if you want, but I like to have my left arm running down the inside of my leg to give a bit of extra support. Plus, you are now more directly leaning onto the perpendicular drill.

Hunker down into a compact ball that is fairly comfortable (comfortable for a firemaking ball that is) and pick up the firebow. Check that string. Is it too loose? Untie, tighten and tie again. I like mine to be fairly tight with just a little bit of tension on the wooden bow. You'll be getting a bunch more tension once that drill is in there and you're working so don't worry about that. Hold it in your hand so that you can control tension with your thumb and first finger as in *photo 13*. Now is a good time for that nose grease but be VERY, VERY careful to remember which end is the grease end! Put the grease end into the fireboard and you might as well cut yourself another hole! Wind the string around the drill as in *photo 15* so that the grease end is upright. Immediately place the top of the drill in the hand cup and lower the whole thing to the fireboard and put the bottom of the drill into the notch.

Make one last body wiggle to get just right in your position.... bring the feet a little closer together, arms in tighter and a little straighter posture..... Now everything is where it's supposed to be and you're good to go!

A hush falls over the crowd....... The clock counts down

3..... 2..... 1!

And you start sawing!

SLOWLY!

I know, I know, you want to rush on after all this and have a huge fire in 5 seconds.... well, it ain't gonna happen like that! Go real slow and concentrate on keeping the drill perpendicular to the fireboard. Focus on rhythmic sawing motions that go from one end of the bow all the way to the other end with even controlled strokes. Always keep the drill revolving in the hole and don't stop. I like to think of what you are doing now as warming up the drill, the hole and the fireboard with heat that will slowly extend further and further from the point of all the action. Try getting your rhythm down and sawing slowly anywhere from 30 seconds to a full minute.... Congratulations! You are now in Stage 1!

Stage 1 - During this stage, you may notice that your drill spins very easy in the socket due to the roughness that you left when carving the drill tip and cutting out the hole.... Don't get too excited! It'll soon be gone and you'll discover a strange grabbing sensation as the drill and hole mate accompanied by a change in sound. Look down at the notch and around the hole and you will probably see the smallest bit of black powder beginning to collect. Excellent! You have just begun Stage 2!

Stage 2 - Pat yourself on the back and focus again on keeping everything in position and your speed stable. Continue for 30 more seconds or maybe a minute.... this is a hard one to estimate as different woods affect the speed of this process. Better to just tell you the changes you will be looking for indicating you are at the doorstep of Stage 3.

Stage 3
See the powder?

Stage 3 - Now you suddenly notice that black powder is grinding out a little more frequently, the drill seems to move a bit easier in the hole and maybe.... just maybe you see the first appearance of a small wisp of smoke drifting from the board..... YEAH!!! Keep going just like you are..... the notch will now start to fill with black powder and smoke will engulf the fireboard, drill and even your hands!

YES!!

This is the easiest time to get too excited and go too fast..... Just keep your head, follow your rhythm and fill that notch with black powder. Once you think that there is a solid stream of smoke coming from THE NOTCH.... NOT THE DRILL AND HOLE, you are at Stage 4 and ready to stop with the drill. VERY CAREFULLY lift the drill from the hole, move your foot from the fireboard and get ready to turn that smoke into fire!

Stage 4 - Take a glance down at your fireboard.... is the smoke still coming from the notch? If not, you probably ended too soon and will have to start over. We'll think positive here and assume you have a strong stream of smoke coming from the notch. The job now is to get the smoking coal into the tinder bundle. I like to use a small stick or pine needle to VERY GENTLY push the smoking coal into the bundle. If you successfully complete this....

CONGRATULATIONS! YOU ARE NEARLY THERE!

Ever so carefully pick up your tinder bundle with the smoking coal in it and gently fold the bundle around the coal. Don't fold too tight, just fold it firmly together.

Stage 5 - Now you will blow your smoking tinder bundle into flame and YEP, this will be dramatic! Start with blowing a soft, gentle stream of air right into the bundle.... beware of blowing too hard or for too long. In general, 5 seconds of air should be enough.

NOW WAIT.

Stage 5 See the smoke?

Give it about 5-10 seconds for the coal to heat up some more of the surrounding tinder and then gently blow again. At this point if all is going well, your smoke will be increasing and getting denser. Great! Now is a good time to start moving toward the tipi you made for the fire. What tipi, you ask? *(photo 16)* Why the one you made before you even started, of course! Soon, in a few more puffs, your entire tinder bundle will burst into flames and you should be holding it right by the tipi and ready to put it in the spot you prepared.

Get ready....
here it comes!

See **The Fire!** section if you need tips on making a good tipi.

Constant movement = increasing heat.
No motion = rapid cooling.

Stage 5 Close to flame!

WARNING!

Don't forget to make a very, very large clearing around your fire making location - Wind can always blow embers away extremely quickly so be ready! I like to keep lots of water nearby and have about 2 feet of cleared dirt around the tipi. I try to keep about 15 to 20 feet around the tipi clear of easily ignitable stuff! Don't forget that pine needles and grass or leaves may smolder underfoot and spread a fire without you even knowing it!

Photo 16 - Fire Tipi

The Fire!

Any good firemaker must have skills at making a good tipi to receive their flaming tinder bundle or all their hard work will be for nothing! Have a fire tipi already set up with tiny twigs in the middle and bigger ones towards the outside...

First - I know..... we have said this before... but it is important! Think safety! Make a large area cleared of flammables and not on a surface that could hold smoldering heat for long (Thick layers of leaves or pine needles are bad!).

Second - Have a spot for different sizes of kindling near your tipi. Sizes should range from the very tiny to the final logs you hope to burn. Once the fire is really going I partially encircle it with some of the larger logs to gradually heat them up.

Third - I like a strong stick in the middle of my tipi, something the thickness of my pinky that I will rest other thinner sticks against. I start leaning more and more thin sticks (drinking straw size and smaller) around the center stick but leave one small four inch area free of these sticks. In this area I will build the home for the tinder bundle.

Fourth - Since my tinder bundle will be tossed in the small area I left open, I'll put the smallest fluff that I can on the bottom and the thinnest twigs that I can around it. Maybe even a spare tinder bundle could go in there. The idea is to put the thinnest, most flammable twigs in this area so your fragile young fire has lots to work with!

The Spirit!

relax... really relax!

I like to go sooooo slowly and picture heat just building and building in that little fireboard hole and the surrounding wood. Breathe. Get a good pace going. Think of how much you will be enjoying your first fire created by your own hands! This may be the single most important thing to remember while you are actually creating the fire. A little respect, a little reflection, some excitement and a bit of anticipation are all you need!

The Practice

or Are-you-having-Troubles?

Q - Hey! My drill keeps slipping! I'm holding the firebow right.... but I can't keep tension on the string! What can I do?

A - Check to see if you have any grooves on drill... if you do, and your drill is thick enough, you need to carefully whittle them off and return your drill to a smooth round shape. Your firebow may also be too flexible... if it seems that the bow is changing shape as you are working, it is probably too flexible. Take the drill out of the string.... does the string droop and sag? If it does, you will need to tie it over - it is too loose! Also review the earlier photos to see the proper hand position as this may affect your firemaking attempts.

Q - My drill keeps popping out of the hole!

A - Many things may cause this but usually you are not keeping the correct pressure pushing down with the hand cup or the notch in your fireboard is too shallow or too close to the edge. Try pushing harder or working slower and the hole will deepen or just make a new hole in the fireboard.

Q - Why does my string keep loosening?

A - It just does! If the string is new it will loosen a lot - once the string has been used for a few fires it will loosen less..... but it will always need to be tied over and over again.

Q - That string wants to run off the top or bottom of drill when sawing... it won't stay in the middle!

A - Your drill is most likely tapered meaning that it is not the same thickness at the top as it is at the bottom. You can either try to whittle it into shape or try a new drill. Also keep in mind that as you are sawing you want to keep your hand level and not angling up or down.

Q - My hand that holds the hand cup keeps wobbling!

A - Check your body position and keep your hand and arm firmly pressed against your shin. Also make sure your foot is within an inch of the fireboard hole.

Q - Uhhh.... my hand cup is burning!

A - Rub that nose and get some more grease happening on the end of the drill..... OR....... Did you put the wrong end into the fireboard hole? If so, make a new hole!

Q - I stopped for maybe 20 seconds and now it feels like I have to start all over again!

A - Yep. Can't let it cool!

Q - I'm exhausted!

A - Make sure you are not doing a bunch of short strokes with your firebow - make them long and from end to end of the firebow. Check out **The Spirit** section and don't get discouraged... it IS exhausting!

Q - Why can't I get an coal to form or fall?

A - Hopefully this is just because your notch is too narrow and you can cut it a little wider. If you really think that you see a coal in the notch, try this! Otherwise you may just be using materials that are not very good for making coals and starting fires. You'll know this if you are getting very little black powder for all your efforts...... Try something else!

Q - I have a great ember but can't get it to burst into fire.

A - Great! Keep in mind that you don't want to blow too hard or too often and if this doesn't help, try different materials for your tinder.

Plants That Work!

Here's my list of preferred plants... I have included plants that I know work because I have used them and you will find their names italicized. The other plants listed here are ones that friends have used or my research has revealed to be usable. Lastly, many of these plants make a good food or have medicinal uses so get a few good guides to positively key them out if you want to try them!

Yucca (Yucca ssp.) In Southern California it is better known as Yucca whipplei and it's also one of my favorites that I use most often. I love yucca string for its ease of creation, plentiful availability and long lasting strength. I'm willing to bet that its botanical cousins could be used similarly and I have heard that it also makes a good fireboard though I haven't tried that yet. Many also swear that it is THE drill making material.... I believe it but our Yucca whipplei is probably not the species most use.

Stinging Nettle (Urtica holosericea and ssp.) A good one for twisting fine cordage from the old stalks. Careful in nettle country - the stings from the fresh plant can range from mildly unpleasant to very painful and long lasting! Sometimes I also include little bits and pieces of old nettle string into my tinder bundle - Does it help a ton? I don't know but it sure doesn't hurt!

Cottonwood (Populus fremontii & ssp.) is used for an awesome fireboard and the inner bark for the best tinder! You can also use small straight branches for the drill and they usually work great! This plant is my favorite for tinder and a fireboard!

Mulefat (Baccharis glutinosa) makes for a great drill and a firebow. Besides, while you are looking for cottonwood you may be walking right through a bunch of these along the creek shore. Find yourself a few branches and give them a try!

Oak (Quercus ssp.) A "punky" oak branch is one of my best fireboards that I have ever had even though it goes against what most will recommend. "Punky" refers to the wood becoming lighter and softer - basically a result of exposure and age. Don't be afraid to try something if it seems like it will work!

Chamise (Adenostoma fasciculatum) makes an OK drill but it seems quirky. Some branches I get work great... others seem to be as hard as rock. Hmmmm... don't know what else to tell you about this one. Some say that it makes a great hand cup and that I believe. Now if only I could remember this the next time I have a super hard piece!

Incense Cedar (Calocedrus or Libocedrus decurrens) A great fireboard! Very soft and easy to work with but usually found in higher elevations (up to 8000 feet).

Elderberry (Sambucus mexicana) can be used for the drill or the fireboard. All I have is word of mouth and a few references on this one. Elderberry is quite famous in Native American living skills and musical studies but I have never used it in firemaking in any way. It has a reputation (a very small reputation) as a fireboard and a drill. I suppose it could work.... this one just gives me the feeling that it would be too much work to be successful and I can't muster that extra work when there are so many other better choices out there!

Milkweed (Asclepias fascicularis & ssp.) The mentioned species has a great abundance of silky fluff in the pods, which are found on the plant in early summer and fall (other species often have similar characteristics). This fluff, much like cattail fluff, is said to be used as tinder to capture and gently nurse a coal into flame. You could also try the fibers found on the dead stalks... the really dead stalks..... you know, the ones that are literally falling apart? These very same fibers in a plant that has recently passed on can be harvested and used to make cordage. Need a bowstring that very instant? This plant could provide you with one if you have real patience and the skill of turning fibers into string!

Soaproot or **Amole** (Chlorogalum ssp.) is a fibrous bulb that is probably a good tinder... Did you catch that I said probably? That's right.... it's covered in thick fibers that become slender wisps at the end and it's readily found (underground that is) in

Southern California - Ventura county in particular..... Crunch some up real fine, make a little ball and I bet it could catch a coal! Also known as a fish stunner, great soap substitute and a starchy food!

Dogbane (Apocynum androsaemifolium & ssp.) WOW! This sucker can make an awesome string! Fantastic! Strong and durable! I think of it as a cousin to stinging nettle. I'm not saying that it is a close botanical cousin.... cause it ain't. But it is prepared and has uses most similar to that plant. Great, great string and fair tinder.... did I mention that it makes great cordage? Yeah, yeah, I know!

Willow (Salix ssp.) often makes a good firebow.... but you will have to experiment. It's often hard to figure out exactly which species of willow you have in your hand ready to turn into a bow. You may want to bend it a bit before deciding.... many willow species are often too flexible!

Cattail (Typha ssp.) is said to make good drills from the stalks, tinder from the flowering head and even cordage. I haven't tried cattail for a drill and I can't really see our local Ventura county cattails working too good for that... and I can't see the cordage from the leaves being strong enough for all that vigorous motion either.... but I do toss the fluff in with my tinder sometimes... Does the fluff from the flowering heads make a great tinder all alone? That I haven't tried but maybe augmented with a bit of grass or finely ground up leaves it could do the trick! On the fun side, it's great entertainment to take handfuls of the fluff and chuck them at your buddies standing by! Some say it's tough to be my friend.......

Oak galls (Quercus ssp.) - You've seen these things before.... remember finding a round baseball sized thing on the ground when walking through a beautiful ancient oak forest? Or maybe you have seen them up in the trees, an odd swelling on the branches... Well, these are also said to be great little tinders.... Just break it open, ground up the insides a bit and set the whole thing under your fireboard. I haven't tried it yet but it's at the top of my list of things that should work.... at the very least it will make moving your coal around easier!

Doug's Suggested Firemaking Kit

What would I suggest if you were just starting out and wanted to get all the odds in your favor?
Check out this list!

Fireboard of cottonwood.

Tinder from the inner bark of an old, old cottonwood. Make sure this tinder is as dry as dry can be! And toss a leaf under it for moving your inevitable coal around.

Drill - A good straight branch of mulefat or cottonwood would do.... I would choose a very, very dry one for this.

String from your boot. No, seriously.... I would try those leather boot shoelaces (real cow leather, not fake) that you can buy in most markets. See the section on string if you are not sure what I am referring to and want to see some.

Firebow of mulefat or willow. This could be either a fresh or dried branch. I have had success with both but the most important factor to consider is how much it bends.

Hand Cup suitably created and greased up from a split piece of oak. (I just can't bring myself to suggest a shot glass!)

Good Luck!

The author of this little guide is a Southern California naturalist that has developed and delivered a variety of natural science and history programs. Since 1988 these hands-on presentations have ranged from monarch butterflies, the gold rush era, tidepools, tracking and desert ecosystems to wilderness survival skills, edible plants, birds of prey, geology and the California Condor.

If you enjoyed this guide....
check out

www.Badgerclaws.com

Mysterious Relics, Treasures, Educational Books and Naturalist Supplies

Here you will find tools for teachers and materials designed to bring a hands-on learning experience to your group or school!

Firemaking Kit

One Firebow   Rawhide String
Two Tinder Bundles   One Hand Cup
One Fireboard

This kit makes a great companion with this guide and all items are created for use!